W9-CFB-778

The Primary Source Library of Famous Composers™

Franz Joseph
Haydn

Eric Michael Summerer

The Rosen Publishing Group's
PowerKids Press™
PRIMARY SOURCE

New York

To Stefanie

Published in 2006 by The Rosen Publishing Group, Inc.
29 East 21st Street, New York, NY 10010

First Edition

Editor: Frances E. Ruffin
Book Design: Michael J. Caroleo
Photo Researcher: Rebecca Anguin-Cohen

Eric "Michaels" Summerer is music director and "morning guy" at the Internet radio station Beethoven.com.

Photo Credits: Cover (Haydn), pp. 12 (bottom), 16, 27 © Erich Lessing/Art Resource, NY; cover and interior borders (sheet music), p. 24 (top) Library of Congress, Music Division; pp. 4, 23, 15 (inset) The Art Archive/Museum der Stadt Wien/Dagli Orti (A); p. 7 (top) © Michael Maslan Historic Photographs/Corbis; pp. 7 (bottom), 15 (bottom) Private Collection/Bridgeman Art Library; p. 8 Palacio Real de Madrid, Spain/Bridgeman Art Library; p. 11 The Art Archive/Osterreichisches Galerie, Vienna/Harper Collins Publishers; p. 12 (inset) The Art Archive/Museo Bibliografico Musicale Bologna/Dagli Orti (A); p. 19 © Archivo Iconografico, S.A./Corbis; pp.20–21 The Art Archive/Nicolas Sapieha; p. 21 (right) Deutsches Theatermuseum, Munich, Germany/Bridgeman Art Library; p. 24 (bottom) Hulton Archive/Getty Images.

Library of Congress Cataloging-in-Publication Data

Summerer, Eric Michael.
Franz Joseph Haydn / Eric Michael Summerer.
     p. cm. — (Primary source library of famous composers)
Includes bibliographical references (p.   ) and index.
Summary: A biography of the composer who became known as the "father of the symphony" after creating more than one hundred in his lifetime.
ISBN 1-4042-2767-9 (library binding)
1. Haydn, Joseph, 1732–1809—Juvenile literature. 2. Composers—Austria—Biography—Juvenile literature. [1. Haydn, Joseph, 1732–1809. 2. Composers.] I. Title. II. Series.
ML3930.H3S8 2005
780'.92—dc22
                              2003018672

Manufactured in the United States of America

Contents

1	Papa Haydn	5
2	A Simple Beginning	6
3	Leaving Home	9
4	To Vienna	10
5	On His Own	13
6	The Perfect Job	14
7	An Unhappy Love	17
8	The Symphony Orchestra	18
9	Eszterháza	20
10	A New Beginning	22
11	Surprise!	25
12	Back to the Family	26
13	Papa Haydn's Legacy	28
	Listening to Haydn/Timeline	29
	Musical Terms	30
	Glossary	31
	Index/Primary Sources/Web Sites	32

Papa Haydn

Franz Joseph Haydn (pronounced HY-din) was one of the greatest **classical music composers** of the eighteenth century. He was born to a poor family and grew up to become a world-famous composer. Many people call him the Father of the **Symphony**. Haydn wrote more than 100 of these long musical pieces, which are played by an **orchestra**. This was a huge amount of music to write. Ludwig van Beethoven, another important composer who lived at the same time as Haydn, wrote only nine symphonies. Other **musicians** loved working with Haydn. They liked him so much that they called him Papa Haydn. By the end of his life, Papa Haydn had helped to change the world of classical music forever.

Franz Joseph Haydn, shown composing in his studio, was hard working, fair, and true to the people who hired him. In fact, he spent almost half of his life in the same job.

A Simple Beginning

Haydn was born on March 31, 1732. His family lived in Rohrau, Austria. Rohrau is a small town near the Hungarian border. His father, Mathias, was a wheelwright. He repaired the wheels of **vehicles**. He also made sure that all of the town's roads, which were **unpaved**, could be traveled on. Haydn's mother was a cook for a wealthy family. Joseph, as Haydn was called, was one of the family's six children who lived to become adults. He had two brothers and three sisters. All three boys became musicians.

Haydn's father loved to play music. He sang **folk songs** with his family while he played the **harp**. Young Haydn pretended to play the **violin** by using two sticks of wood. He held one under his chin and used the other as the bow. At that time his family could only dream of giving him real music lessons.

Top: *Austria is the land of Haydn's birth.*
Bottom: *Haydn was born in this farmhouse in Rohrau, Austria.*

Leaving Home

When Haydn was six, his uncle Johann Mathias Franck came to visit. Franck ran a boys' school in the nearby town of Hainburg. He also played the **organ** in the church there. He liked to watch Joseph pretend to play a violin and to hear him sing. Franck offered to teach Joseph at his school. Haydn's parents could not afford a good education for him at home, so they agreed to send him away to school. For many years, Haydn rarely saw his parents. Franck was a tough teacher. Every day Joseph and his classmates got up early in the morning. They had three hours of schoolwork, during which they learned the Latin language, writing, and math. Then they went to church. After lunch they had three more hours of classes.

In eighteenth-century European classrooms, such as the one shown here, students learned to read and to write with a pen made of a feather.

After lunch Joseph and his classmates had three more hours of school. They took lessons to learn the violin and the keyboard, an instrument that is played with keys.

To Vienna

Shortly after Joseph's eighth birthday, a man named Georg Reutter visited Joseph's school. He was looking for boys to sing in the St. Stephen's **Cathedral choir** school in Vienna, the capital of Austria. As soon as Reutter heard Joseph sing, he asked him to join the famous choir. This was a huge honor. In Vienna, Joseph learned more about music and the world around him. Joseph sang in the church choir for nine years. He was asked to leave at the age of 17. Some people believe he left because his voice had become deeper, and he could not sing high notes anymore. One story, however, says that he was asked to leave for cutting the pigtail off the wig of the boy in front of him.

Reutter was not kind to the boys. They were often very hungry. Haydn later said that he liked to sing at important parties because that was the only time he got a good meal.

Haydn sang in the choir of St. Stephen's Cathedral in Vienna, shown here, from the age of eight. The church was built in 1147, and the tower was completed in 1433.

On His Own

Suddenly, Haydn was on his own in the big city of Vienna. Somehow he had to earn a living. He played music on the street and gave music lessons to wealthy families. He continued to study music written by famous composers. He also began to write his own **compositions**. He gave them to his students to play. One of Haydn's students was the daughter of Italian poet Pietro Metastasio, who was famous for writing the lyrics, or words, to **operas**. She also took singing lessons from the great Italian singer and composer Niccolo Porpora. This connection proved lucky for Haydn. Porpora offered to give Haydn lessons in composing music. In exchange for lessons Haydn did odd jobs, such as shining Porpora's shoes. Haydn also learned to speak Italian. Metastasio and Porpora helped Haydn to get his next job.

Haydn took an apartment in Vienna's Kohlmarkt, a busy market place. Inset: Niccolo Porpora, who became Haydn's teacher, lived from 1686 to 1766.

The Perfect Job

Prince Nikolaus played the baryton, which is a cross between a guitar and a violin. Haydn learned to play the baryton, but Nikolaus became angry that Haydn played the baryton better than he could!

In the eighteenth century, the best way for a musician to make money was to work in the **court** of an **aristocrat**, such as a prince or other royalty. Many aristocrats had their own orchestras in their palaces. This allowed them to hear new music whenever they wanted. Haydn was lucky enough to find one of these jobs. When Haydn was 29 years old, he met Prince Paul Anton Esterházy, a Hungarian nobleman. Esterházy offered him a job as music director at Eisenstadt Castle. The estate was 30 miles (48 km) from Vienna. Haydn would live in the family castle, and he would be in charge of the orchestra there. When the prince died, Haydn worked for Paul Anton's brother, Nikolaus. Nikolaus was also a musician, and he treated Haydn well.

Haydn may have taught music to these Esterházy children. Inset: Prince Nikolaus Esterházy was known as Nikolaus the Magnificent.

An Unhappy Love

Around the time that Haydn went to work at Eisenstadt Castle he fell in love with a young woman named Therese Keller. He wanted to marry her, but, before she met him, she had planned to enter a **convent** and become a nun. As a nun, Therese could not marry. Her parents offered to let Haydn marry her older sister, Maria Anna, which he did in 1760. She was 31, and he was 28. It was not a happy marriage. She did not seem to care that Haydn was a great composer. Some people claimed that she lined a baking pan with sheets of his music. According to the stories, she also cut the paper into strips to use to curl her hair. To make things worse, Therese left the convent. By then it was too late. Haydn and Maria Anna were already married. During their 40-year marriage, the couple never had children.

This photo of Haydn's room at Eisenstadt shows sheets of his music and the "servants'" coat that he was made to wear while in the castle. Inset: This is a painting of Haydn's wife, Maria Anna.

The Symphony Orchestra

Haydn's steady job gave him a place to live and plenty to eat. Not having to worry about money allowed him to spend all of his energy on writing music. He spent most of his time writing symphonies. When Haydn first began to compose, most symphonies were short, simple works played at the beginning of operas. Haydn wrote symphonies that were longer and more interesting.

A symphony is played with different kinds of instruments in an orchestra. At first, Haydn's orchestra was very small, with only about 12 musicians. As he became more famous, fine musicians from all over Europe wanted to be in his orchestra. Haydn wrote music for larger groups of instruments. Soon about 30 people played in his orchestra. Today a symphony orchestra has about 100 musicians.

The color engraving shows Joseph Haydn leading musicians. An engraving is art that is cut into wood or some other surface and then printed.

Eszterháza

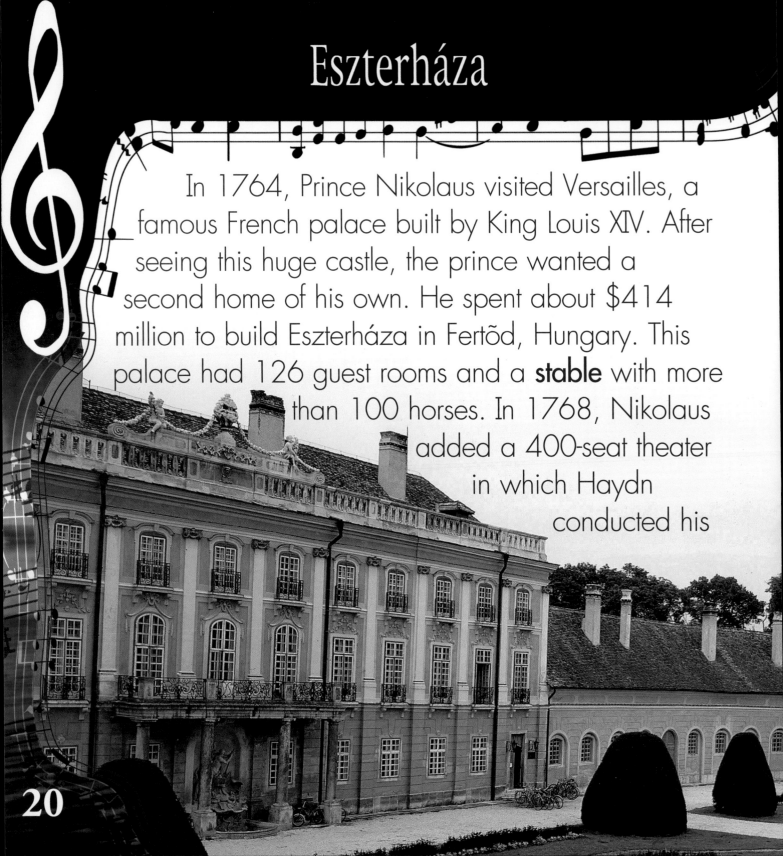

In 1764, Prince Nikolaus visited Versailles, a famous French palace built by King Louis XIV. After seeing this huge castle, the prince wanted a second home of his own. He spent about $414 million to build Eszterháza in Fertõd, Hungary. This palace had 126 guest rooms and a **stable** with more than 100 horses. In 1768, Nikolaus added a 400-seat theater in which Haydn conducted his

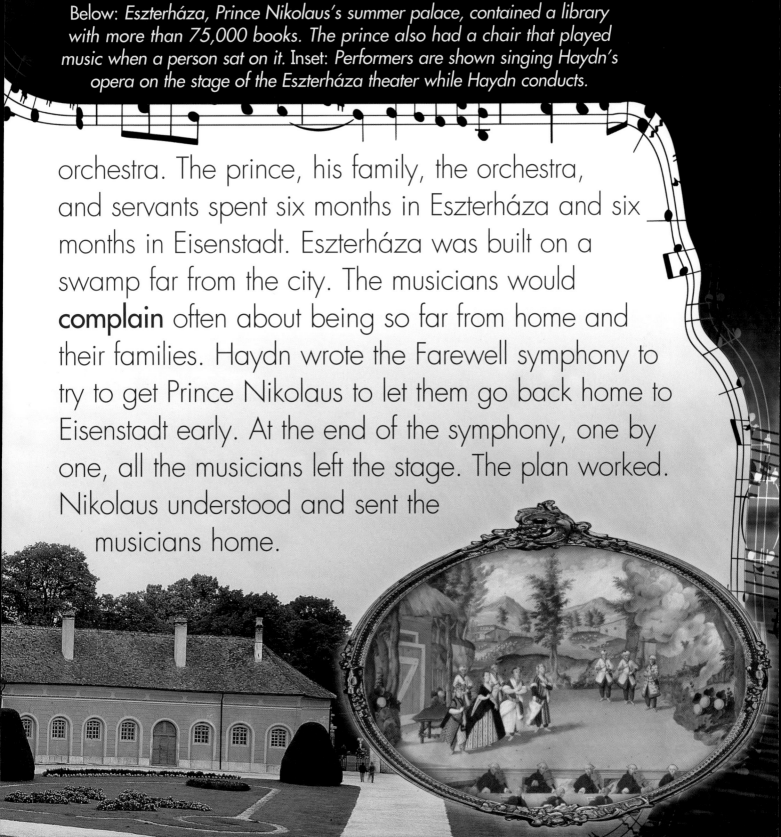

Below: *Eszterháza, Prince Nikolaus's summer palace, contained a library with more than 75,000 books. The prince also had a chair that played music when a person sat on it. Inset: Performers are shown singing Haydn's opera on the stage of the Eszterháza theater while Haydn conducts.*

orchestra. The prince, his family, the orchestra, and servants spent six months in Eszterháza and six months in Eisenstadt. Eszterháza was built on a swamp far from the city. The musicians would **complain** often about being so far from home and their families. Haydn wrote the Farewell symphony to try to get Prince Nikolaus to let them go back home to Eisenstadt early. At the end of the symphony, one by one, all the musicians left the stage. The plan worked. Nikolaus understood and sent the musicians home.

A New Beginning

Prince Nikolaus died in 1790, when Haydn was 58 years old. Nikolaus's son Anton, the new ruler, did not want his own orchestra, so the musicians had to find new work. However, he continued to pay Haydn part of his old salary. Haydn could have settled down to a quiet **retirement**, but he still wanted to compose music. In 1791, Haydn's friend Johann Peter Solomon, a violinist, invited him to London, England. An excited Haydn accepted the invitation. While he was in London, Haydn held **concerts** of his music, and he composed a number of very popular symphonies. He made friends with many important people, such as the Prince of Wales, who later became George IV, king of England. Haydn received an **honorary degree** from Oxford **University**. Haydn and his music were much loved in England.

This engraving shows Haydn on the boat to London, England. When Haydn left for this trip, he did not speak English.

"THE SURPRISE"

ANDANTE FROM HAYDN'S SYMPHONY

No 3.

Transcribed by
WM. VINCENT WALLACE.

Surprise!

While he was in London, Haydn enjoyed a friendly musical **competition** with a former student named Ignaz Pleyel. Both men took turns writing symphonies, each one trying to compose one better than the other's. The English enjoyed this, because they got to hear a lot of new pieces. The piece that finally won the **contest** was Haydn's Symphony No. 94 in G Major, the Surprise symphony. As the story goes, Haydn wrote a nice, **soothing** second movement that sounds a little like the song "Twinkle Twinkle Little Star." About 30 seconds into the piece, however, just as some people might be falling asleep, the whole orchestra plays loudly all at once, "BUUUUUM!" Surprise!

Many of Haydn's symphonies are named after what they sound like. Their names include the Hunt, the Bear, the Clock, the Hen, and the Drumroll.

The andante, or slow movement, of Haydn's Surprise symphony comes before the "surprise." Inset: This is a popular engraving of Haydn.

25

Back to the Family

In 1795, at the age of 63, Haydn returned to the Esterházy family. The new prince, Nikolaus Esterházy II, wanted to have his own orchestra. However, he did not like music that did not include singing. Every year, he asked Haydn to write a **choral Mass**. Haydn worked for the family until 1802, when he became ill. He had worked for the Esterházy family off and on for about 40 years. The last time Haydn was seen in public was at a **performance** of his *Mass Creation* to celebrate his seventy-sixth birthday. When it was over the **audience** cheered so much that Haydn burst into tears. After this event, his health grew worse. On May 31, 1809, Haydn died at the age of 77. He had a simple **funeral**. However, Franz Joseph Haydn, known as the Father of the Symphony, will be remembered for a long time to come.

In this watercolor painting, the audience was very moved by listening to a performance of Haydn's Creation Mass shortly before his death.

Papa Haydn's Legacy

Haydn's style can be heard in the music of nearly every classical composer that came after him. Beethoven and Mozart listened to the way he composed, and they created their music based on his ideas. Many other composers wrote their music using the ideas of Beethoven and Mozart. However, much of their music can be traced back to Franz Joseph Haydn.

Today you can hear Haydn's music almost everywhere. In 1922, Germany adopted Haydn's "Emperor's **Hymn**" and used the music from this composition as its national **anthem**. Whenever a German athlete wins a gold medal in the Olympics and the "Emperor's Hymn" is played, we all can remember Papa Haydn.

Listening to Haydn

Trumpet Concerto in E-flat Major
The trumpet was a new instrument when Haydn
wrote this concerto.
Symphony No. 45 in F-sharp Minor, The Farewell
At the end of this symphony, one by one, each member of the
orchestra stops playing and walks off the stage.
Symphony No. 94 in G Major, The Surprise
The "surprise" comes about 30 seconds into the second movement.
Symphony No. 101 in D, The Clock
This symphony is named for the "tick-tock" sound that you can
hear in the second movement.

Timeline

1732 Franz Joseph Haydn is born in Rohrau, Austria, on March 31.
1740 Haydn joins the choir at St. Stephen's in Vienna.
1760 Haydn and Maria Anna Keller marry.
1761 Haydn begins work for the Esterházy family.
1772 Haydn composes the Farewell symphony.
1790 Prince Nikolaus dies, and Haydn goes to London.
1791 Haydn composes the Surprise symphony.
1793 Haydn travels to Vienna to teach Beethoven to compose music.
1809 Haydn dies at the age of 77 in Vienna on May 31.

Musical Terms

anthem (AN-thum) A blessed or an official song or hymn.

choir (KWYR) A group of people who sing together.

choral (KOR-ul) Involving a choir or chorus.

classical music (KLA-sih-kul MYOO-zik) Music in the style of the eighteenth and nineteenth centuries.

composers (kom-POH-zerz) People who write music.

compositions (kom-puh-ZIH-shunz) Pieces of writing or music.

concerts (KON-serts) Public musical performances.

folk songs (FOHK SONGZ) Traditional songs of a region or of a country.

harp (HARP) A musical instrument consisting of a frame with strings that must be plucked.

hymn (HIM) Songs of praise that honor God.

Mass (MAS) A musical piece based on a church service.

musicians (myoo-ZIH-shunz) People who write, play, or sing music.

operas (AH-pruhz) Forms of theater in which the story is told through singing.

orchestra (OR-kes-truh) A group of people who play music together.

organ (OR-gen) A keyboard instrument that makes music by driving air through pipes of different sizes.

symphony (SIM-fuh-nee) A long musical composition written for an orchestra.

violin (vy-uh-LIN) A small instrument that makes sound by having a bow drawn over its strings.

Glossary

aristocrat (uh-RIS-tuh-krat) A member of the wealthy upper class.

audience (AH-dee-ints) A group of people who watch or listen to something.

cathedral (kuh-THEE-drul) A large church that is run by a bishop.

competition (kom-pih-TIH-shin) A game or test.

complain (kum-PLAYN) To express feelings of pain or dissatisfaction.

contest (KON-test) A game or test.

convent (KON-vent) A place where nuns live.

court (KORT) The king, queen, or other ruler's advisers and officers.

funeral (FYOON-rul) A service held when burying the dead.

honorary degree (AH-neh-rer-ee duh-GREE) A rank or title given by a college or a university as an honor.

performance (per-FOR-mens) The giving of a play, circus act, or other show.

retirement (ree-TYR-ment) The giving up of an office or other career.

soothing (SOOTH-ing) Calming.

stable (STAY-bul) The building in which horses are sheltered and fed.

university (yoo-nih-VER-sih-tee) A school of higher education that is made up of one or more colleges.

unpaved (un-PAYVD) Not covered with a hard human-made surface.

vehicles (VEE-uh-kulz) Means of moving or carrying things.

Index

B
Beethoven, Ludwig van, 5, 28

C
choir, 10

E
Eisenstadt Castle, 14, 17, 21
Esterházy, Paul Anton, 14
Esterházy, Nikolaus, 14, 20–22
Esterházy, Nikolaus II, 26
Eszterháza, 20–21

F
Franck, Johann Mathias, 9

H
Haydn, Mathias (father), 6

K
Keller, Maria Anna, 17
Keller, Therese, 17

L
London, England, 22, 25

M
Mass, 26
Metastasio, Pietro, 13

O
operas, 13

P
Pleyel, Ignaz, 25
Porpora, Niccolo, 13

R
Reutter, Georg, 10
Rohrau, Austria, 6

S
school, 9–10
Solomon, Johann Peter, 22
symphony(ies), 5, 18, 21–22, 25

V
Vienna, Austria, 10, 13–14

Primary Sources

Cover. Portrait of Franz Joseph Haydn painted by Thomas Bush Hardy (1842–1897), Royal Academy of Arts, London.
Page 7. An 1826 map of Austria shows settlements, district boundaries, roads, and topographical features. Created in 1826 by Joseph Perkins.
Page 8. *Interior of a Schoolroom*, an oil on canvas painting by French artist Michel-Ange Houasse (1680–1730). Palacio Real de Madrid, Spain.
Page 11. St. Stephen's Cathedral, Vienna, by Stephen Alt (1832).
Page 12. The Kohlmarkt, in Vienna in 1786, a painting by Carl Schuetz (1838–1923), Historisches Museum der Stadt Wien, Vienna.
Page 15. *Three Children Seated on a Sofa*, an oil on canvas painting of three Esterházy children. By Johann Georg Weikert (1745–1799).
Page 16, inset. Miniature painting of Haydn's wife, Maria Anna Aloysia Haydn. Possibly painted by Ludwig Gutenbrunn, Haydn Museum, Eisenstadt.
Page 21. Haydn conducting the first performance of his opera *L'Incontro Improvviso!* ("An Unexpected Meeting!") at the Eszterháza Theater, 1775. By German School, eighteenth century.
Page 24. Sheet music of the Andante movement from Haydn's Surprise Symphony, No. 3.
Page 24, inset. A nineteenth-century engraving by F.A. Andorff after C. Jaeger.

Web Sites

Due to the changing nature of Internet links, PowerKids Press has developed an online list of Web Sites related to the subject of this book. This site is updated regularly. Please use this link to access the list:
www.powerkidslinks.com/plfc/haydn/